STARVED

THE **MERCY FOR** SERIES

STARVED

Mercy for Eating Disorders

NANCY ALCORN

WINEPRESS **WP** PUBLISHING

WinePress Publishing (PO Box 428, Enumclaw, WA 98022) functions only as book publisher. As such, the ultimate design, content, editorial accuracy, and views expressed or implied in this work are those of the author.

Unless otherwise noted, all Scriptures are taken from the *Holy Bible, New International Version®*, NIV®. Copyright © 1973, 1978, 1984 by the International Bible Society. Used by permission of Zondervan. All rights reserved.

Scripture references marked NLT are taken from the *Holy Bible, New Living Translation*, copyright © 1996, 2004. Used by permission of Tyndale House Publishers, Inc., Wheaton, Illinois 60189. All rights reserved.

Scripture references marked NASB are taken from the New American Standard Bible, © 1960, 1963, 1968, 1971, 1972, 1973, 1975, 1977 by The Lockman Foundation. Used by permission.

Scripture references marked MSG are taken from *THE MESSAGE*, copyright © 1993, 1994, 1995, 1996, 2000, 2001, 2002. Used by permission of NavPress Publishing Group.

Scripture references marked CEV are taken from The Contemporary English Version: Thomas Nelson, © 1997, 1995 by the American Bible Society. Used by permission. All rights reserved.

Scripture references marked AMP are taken from *THE AMPLIFIED BIBLE*, Copyright © 1954, 1958, 1962, 1964, 1965, 1987 by The Lockman Foundation. All rights reserved. Used by permission. (www.Lockman. org)

Scripture references marked NKJV are taken from the New King James Version. Copyright © 1979, 1980, 1983 by Thomas Nelson, Inc. Used by permission. All rights reserved.

ISBN 13: 978-1-57921-898-0
ISBN 10: 1-57921-898-9
Library of Congress Catalog Card Number: 2007921240

ENDORSEMENTS

Our work exposes us to thousands of young women, many of them hurting. We have seen firsthand the work of Mercy Ministries. Inside the *Mercy for . . .* series are many stories of girls finding true healing after years of suffering—read this series for real hope and a lifetime of freedom!

—**BarlowGirl**
Contemporary Christian Recording Artists

I know all too well how the world places an overemphasis on what we see on the outside, and girls often resort to self-destructive patterns. I personally support the work of Mercy Ministries because I have seen firsthand the changed lives.

—**Niki Taylor**
International Supermodel

As a father of two girls in their late teens, I certainly know what girls face today. I have watched Nancy Alcorn and Mercy Ministries bring hope and healing to struggling young women for many years—young women who were completely without hope. The *Mercy for . . .* series reveals the Mercy Ministries difference and offers great inspiration, hope, and a way to true healing for all who want to be free.

—**Dave Ramsey**
Financial Expert and Author of *The Total Money Makeover*

Nancy Alcorn offers young women hope—to have self-esteem and grow in wholeness—and more. Mercy Ministries is not afraid to deal with the tough, ugly stuff. If you are a young woman struggling with these issues, or if you have a daughter or work with girls, you want to hear what Nancy has to say. It is sure to change your life!

—CeCe Winans
Grammy Award-Winning Recording Artist

I have personally known young women who have found healing through the principles in these books. This series is very timely in an age where little hope is given for young women struggling with these issues. Nancy Alcorn is not afraid to tell the truth and offer real hope through forgiveness and restoration. If you are desperate for hope or affected by a hopeless life, read through this series and find real answers.

—Sue Semrau
Head Women's Basketball Coach, Florida State University

DEDICATION

To those who are **desperate** for help
but feel there is no hope.
This book has been placed in your **hands** for a reason—
it is no accident that you are reading this even now.
My **prayer** is that you will read on,
because this book was written for you.
If you receive its message,
you will **never** be the same!

—*Nancy Alcorn*

TABLE OF CONTENTS

ACKNOWLEDGEMENTS

I would like to thank the Mercy Ministries staff who have spent countless hours working on this manuscript with a heart to help people—Sherry Douglas, Cassidy Carlgren, Cissy Etheridge, Janelle Pharis, Ashley Cupples, Amanda Goldsberry, and Sarah Dixon.

Thanks to the Mercy residents who read the manuscripts and provided honest feedback, helping to ensure the most helpful and relevant material.

A heartfelt thanks to our friends and supporters throughout the world who give so generously to bring forth changed lives.

Last but not least, I have such gratitude for our faithful staff in the various homes around the world. They give so much every day, and their love and compassion is evident. Thanks for serving alongside me in this global vision. You guys amaze me!

All royalties and profits from this book will go back into the work of Mercy Ministries around the world.

SPECIAL THANKS . . .

To the young woman pictured on the cover. Thank you for allowing us to use this photo made of you while receiving help for an eating disorder. I am so proud of you for completing the program as an overcomer who is now walking in freedom. May thousands of others follow in your footsteps.

INTRODUCTION

It's all a blur. I am trapped inside my own mind in this obsession with my food and my desire to be thin. It consumes my entire life. My reflection makes me cringe, and the battle within me never stops. I don't want to die, but in this state I refuse to live.

—Allie, personal journal entry

The destruction an eating disorder causes is like a tornado devouring everything in its path. How does the seemingly insignificant desire to lose a few pounds become something so powerful that it demands control of your entire life? Allie, who has struggled with anorexia and bulimia for several years, and her mother provide some insights throughout this book as they describe their fight for Allie's life.

Despite how they often feel, Allie and her mother are not alone in their struggle. Eating disorders are devastating millions of lives across the world, affecting mostly females, but sometimes males too. A 2002 Harvard University study reported that five million people in the United States suffer from eating disorders. Many more cases go unreported as girls struggle in silence. Those with eating disorders surpass their goal to lose a few pounds and progress into an overwhelming addiction, a coping mechanism to deal with the pain of living in a fallen world.

There are many girls, just like you, wanting a way out. Many have found it, and you will read some of their stories. Since 1983, Mercy Ministries has served more than two thousand young women from across the country and from varied cultural and economic backgrounds.

Young women who come to Mercy Ministries are often facing a combination of difficult circumstances, and many of them have sought prior treatment without successful long-term results, yet they graduate from the Mercy Ministries program truly transformed. They are found attending universities, working in ministries and in corporations, on the mission field, and at home raising families. Our residents are young women who want to change and move beyond their difficult circumstances, yet have never been able to before. But at Mercy Ministries, they find hope.

You can find hope too. This book was written to give you more understanding of your struggle and help you learn practical ways to acknowledge, identify, and eliminate an eating disorder from your life. There is hope, there is freedom, and there is mercy for eating disorders.

Chapter One

WHAT ARE EATING DISORDERS?

When a very thin movie star dominates the screen, it's not uncommon to hear "Whoa! She definitely has an eating disorder!" being murmured throughout the audience. *Eating disorder* is a label that is easily slapped on anyone today who looks the least bit unhealthy. But an eating disorder goes far beyond your physical appearance. In fact, you might be struggling with a severe eating disorder that is causing permanent damage to your internal organs, yet never appear sick or underweight.

There are several types of eating disorders. Some girls struggle with one predominately, while others bounce from one type to the next. Regardless of the specific eating disorder, severe and sometimes permanent damage can result from any of them.

Signs and Symptoms

Eating disorders are very common today, but frequently they go undetected due to their secretive nature. It's important to be aware of the signs and symptoms so you can recognize that you yourself have a problem or that someone you know is struggling with a disorder.

Some of these signs and symptoms can have other causes besides an eating disorder, so a medical exam is always a good idea when you are evaluating your situation.

STARVED

Anorexia Nervosa

Anorexia is identified by a severely distorted perception of one's physical appearance. This mind-set leads to actions, including self-starvation and excessive exercise, rooted in an intense fear of gaining weight. Some of the signs and symptoms of anorexia look like this:

Physical: Continual weight loss, irregular periods, dizziness and/or fainting spells, low body temperature (complaining of being cold), pale complexion and dry skin, dry brittle hair or hair that is falling out, growth of facial and fine body hair, easy bruising, exhaustion and fatigue.

Emotional: Intense fear of weight gain, excessive need for control, distorted body image, dramatic mood swings.

Behavioral: Wearing loose clothing, deception (hiding food in napkins or clothes), abuse of laxatives, diet pills, or diuretics, obsession with caloric and fat content of food, compulsive exercise, making excuses not to eat ("I already ate" or "I have an upset stomach"), isolating or avoiding social events, consuming a lot of non-caloric foods (such as diet soda, gum, or coffee), avoiding restaurants and eating in front of others, ritualistic behaviors at meals (such as eating food in a particular order or cutting food into tiny pieces), discomfort with or avoiding being touched, defensiveness when questioned about weight, hyperactivity, and depression.

Bulimia Nervosa

Bulimia is identified by compulsive overeating leading to self-induced vomiting. The abuse of laxatives and diuretics is commonly used in an attempt to purge the body of food. Some of the signs and symptoms of bulimia look like this:

Physical*:* Bingeing and purging, constant sore throat, broken blood vessels in eyes, dramatic weight fluctuation, digestive problems, swollen neck glands and puffy cheeks, scrape wounds on knuckles (due to contact between knuckles and teeth to induce vomiting), eroding of tooth enamel and increased cavities.

Emotional*:* Self-criticism and poor body image, poor impulse control (drugs, alcohol, spending, mood), and promiscuity.

Behavioral*:* Expressing guilt after eating, avoiding restaurants and eating in front of others, abusing laxatives, diet pills, ipecac, diuretics, and/or enemas, frequently going into the bathroom right after meals, showering after meals, hiding food throughout the house, alternating between eating large amounts of food and self-starvation.

Binge-Eating Disorder

Binge-eating is identified by consuming large quantities of food in an uncontrolled manner. Some of the signs and symptoms of binge-eating disorder look like this:

Physical: Rapid weight gain.

Emotional*:* Poor body image, depression, and excessive guilt.

Behavioral*:* Eating large amounts of food, eating late at night, sexual avoidance, hiding food throughout the house, eating to the point of physical discomfort, avoiding social events, eating without an appetite, isolating, and sleeping often during the day.

Medical Consequences

My body is wasting away from the inside out. My doctor is very concerned, but I am far from achieving the results I

desire in my physical appearance. I appear to be holding it together, but I guess my doctor got a glimpse of the truth.
—Allie, personal journal entry

Eating disorders rarely leave the physical body unaffected; there are always consequences to bad choices. Our choices can affect the rest of our lives. Knowing ahead of time where the road you are on is taking you tomorrow may encourage you to evaluate the choices you are making today or your decision to speak to someone else you suspect is in trouble.

Some of the long-term results of eating disorders include: osteoporosis, muscle deterioration, anemia, organ damage, acid reflux, esophageal tears, chronic constipation, abnormal liver function, elevated cholesterol, decreased estrogen, infertility, abnormal blood pressure, heart attack, stroke, brain shrinkage, and death.

Behind the Behavior

The media, fashion industry, and even your family can influence an eating disorder, but more than likely it did not start there. Most eating disorders stem from deep emotional, psychological, and spiritual roots. There are different ways of handling stressful and discouraging events in our lives, but anorexia, bulimia, and binge-eating are not healthy options. So how do eating disorders start, and why do you do fall into these behaviors?

Control

The behaviors associated with an eating disorder make you feel that you are in control. However, just the opposite is true. When you choose to give in to the harmful behaviors of anorexia, bulimia, or binge-eating, you are actually giving control of your life to your enemy, the devil. The enemy wants you to believe that because you can deny yourself food you have some sort of power over your body and over your life. But the Bible says that we are slaves to whatever controls us (2 Peter 2:19).

"Be on the alert. Your adversary, the devil, prowls around like a roaring lion, seeking someone to devour" (1 Peter 5:8, NASB). Satan is your adversary, your enemy. He wants you to believe that you are in control of your life, but this is a deception tactic to keep you in bondage. The way to walk in freedom is to choose to surrender control of your life to God instead of trying to control your life yourself.

> *With everything in my life so out of control, it is easy for me to focus on food. I feel so powerful knowing I can have so much self-control, but it is slowly becoming bigger than me. How has something I thought I owned grown to own me? I can't do it anymore by myself—I need help.*
>
> —Allie's personal journal entry

There are healthier ways than developing and living with an eating disorder to handle your intense emotions. Some of these include praise and worship, prayer, reading the Word of God out loud, journaling, and seeking Christian counseling. Later we will discuss in greater detail the power of speaking God's Word aloud so that you can defeat the devil's attempt to keep you in bondage. Prayer is essential no matter how many other things you choose to do to help you walk in freedom. Here's a sample prayer you can use every day to help you stop trying to control your own life and give control to God:

Prayer of Surrender

Lord, help me to remember that together you and I can handle anything that comes my way today. Instead of giving in to old patterns of coping with overwhelming emotions, I choose to give you control over my life. I ask you to be in charge. I am not willing for my life to stay the same. Today I take this step: to give you control that I may walk through my day in mental, physical, and emotional peace. Until I have developed this choice to the point where it becomes natural to me, please walk with me through every moment of the day. I will make the choice—you will be my strength. In Jesus' name, Amen.

Unhealthy Expressions

Why won't everyone just leave me alone? My family seems more concerned about what I am or am not eating and don't seem to care about me! I am hurting, confused, and feel so alone, but I just don't know how to express it.
                            —Allie, personal journal entry

God gave us the ability to experience feelings, but He doesn't want us to be controlled by our emotions. Your feelings and emotions will find an expression in your life. Make the decision to share them with others in a safe healthy way, so they don't express themselves in destructive patterns with the potential to destroy your life.

It is important to express what you are feeling to someone else with whom you are comfortable. If communicating with words is hard for you, try creative writing, drawing or painting, or journaling. Ensure that you are able to share what is going on with a mature Christian you can trust, someone who can listen and help you to process emotions that may seem overwhelming or out of control.

Anorexia, bulimia, and binge-eating are all used to express emotions through unhealthy behaviors. As you understand the connection between your outside behaviors and how you feel inside, you can begin to get to the root of the eating disorder.

Anorexia can be used to avoid unpleasant emotions or feelings by focusing on food. Even though girls struggling with anorexia are starving themselves, they are typically preoccupied with food. They obsess over calories, health foods, and exercising. This unhealthy obsession is used to escape from unwanted emotions.

Bulimia is often used to express negative emotions or feelings that become too overwhelming to put into words. Through self-induced vomiting or laxative/diuretic abuse, emotions are "purged" out. The temporary release of endorphins misleads you to think this attempt was successful—until the destructive emotional release becomes an overwhelming addiction.

Binge-eating is an actual reflection of emotions that are out of control. Many girls turn to this disorder as an attempt to communicate the chaos they feel inside by acting out of control on the outside. However, what is actually going on is not being communicated, and binge-eating becomes a vicious cycle which leads to hopelessness and shame.

You may not choose the emotions that you feel, but you do have a choice about what you do with those emotions. As you choose to express how you are feeling in healthy ways, you are also choosing freedom. Becoming free is a very slow process, and at first you need to include a lot of accountability and support. Do not give in to your fear of rejection or hesitate to reach out to those around you!

Our emotions rarely remain constant and frequently are not rooted in truth. At times, you have to choose to believe the truth over how you feel in the moment. You may not feel worthy, loved, or accepted unconditionally, but God's truth, which is the ultimate truth, says that you are. Choose to believe it!

Outside Influences

"Your enemy the devil prowls around like a roaring lion looking for someone to devour" (1 Peter 5:8). The devil is cunning and will slither through any door you leave open for him. In today's culture, media—movies, TV, magazines, the Internet—and fashion are doors that Satan easily creeps through. Neither media nor fashion is necessarily a bad thing, but Satan often uses them to distort God's truth about who you are. Movie stars, television icons, and fashion models define beauty and promote the lie that anything less is unacceptable. The irony is that the perfect image doesn't even exist!

It's not wise to isolate yourself from the culture you live in, but it is important to be aware of what is out there. Use wisdom about the outside influences you subject yourself to, and when you are confronted with Satan's distortions, recognize them for what they are and how they may affect you.

Movies, TV, and Magazines

Ashleigh is twenty-two and a mass communications major at a California college. With experience in modeling, as well as being raised in an atmosphere that revolved around the fashion industry, Ashleigh got a firsthand taste of the pressure the media places on girls to portray that "perfect image." She remembers that media, in the forms of television, movies, and magazines, was always a part of her life. "It was always in the house. My dad is a designer, and I would see the models and be very influenced. They would be around, and I would think fashion was cool, but then it came to the point that I wanted to be the people in those magazines. From ages four to seven, I modeled, but when I was old enough to be aware of fashion and to start designing myself, I went from wanting to wear the clothing to wanting to look like the models."

For Ashleigh, this was not only the beginning of a career but also a downward spiral into an obsession that would soon control her life.

The Internet

"Things got worse as I found myself going to the internet all the time," Ashleigh explains.

The Internet has become a prime source of communication, filled with information about almost anything imaginable and opening the door for both positive and negative communication on a global scale. Chat rooms have made communication possible between people from all parts of the world. Girls struggling with eating disorders are naturally drawn to each other in chat rooms, because they feel understood by one another.

The initial attraction between girls with similar circumstances begins innocently enough. They seek support, comfort, and understanding. Who better to understand than girls who share the same struggle? But Satan has gladly distorted this opportunity for hope. Maybe that's one reason why the Bible says, "Avoid godless chatter, because those who indulge in it will become more and more ungodly. Their teaching will spread like gangrene" (2 Timothy 2:16–17). Proverbs 18:21 says, "The tongue has the power of life and death." Chat rooms provide plenty of room for Satan to do his prowling. Know what is out there so that you can be proactive in your fight for freedom.

The Fashion Industry

The fashion industry is filled with girls who are engaged in a dangerous competition over who can be the thinnest, prettiest, sexiest, and most successful. But it is almost impossible to be content with yourself when you are no longer able to appreciate the beauty in others and only see their beauty as a threat.

Ashleigh describes her experience with this aspect of modeling: "I found a job for 'fit modeling.' That's where clothing designers fit a specific size of clothing to your body. They make alterations for that size according to your figure. I went downstairs to the corporate room where they displayed their top model. She was who I had to look like. I remember going in there and thinking that I was fatter than her. The CEO of the company was there and told me, 'You can't gain weight for this job.' So in my mind it clicked that I would just have to not eat. I would go online with my photographs next to those of someone famous, comparing them to see what was not measuring up and what was. I would think that I was still fat and how I wanted to get thinner. I wanted to get prettier, and to me, thinner was prettier."

In her college studies, Ashleigh had an interesting opportunity to explore the lies behind the fashion and modeling industry. Realizing the truth about the pictures and distorted images presented by the media relieves the pressure of having to meet a standard that doesn't exist! "I analyzed an ad with this beautiful woman," Ashleigh explains. "She was very thin and looked very seductive. It wasn't even a real person. Models' faces can be computerized. They put the perfect eyes with the perfect nose, etc. They airbrush the bodies because the women don't really look like that! Being around other models, you can see firsthand that what you see in the media definitely isn't real!"

There's another downside to modeling and the fashion world. It hurts to feel that no one can see past your outer appearance. Yet if that is all you are focused on, how can you expect anyone to see past it? "It was always about how I looked, how pretty I was, how my makeup was done, or what my outfit looked like," says Ashleigh. "No one ever wanted to get real or hear about something on the inside of me."

Ashleigh continues, "They didn't want to know me. I had a lot to share. I went to a great school, and I loved to learn, but at that point it was about how little I could eat and how beautiful I could be. I definitely was not in touch with real life. Through numerous media outlets, the enemy feeds the whole world a lie that how we look is all that matters. It just made me completely lifeless and empty."

What About Pro-Ana?

Pro-ana is a term that has become common among girls looking to the Internet for answers. The prefix *pro* means "in favor of," and *ana* is short for anorexia. (The term *pro-mia* means "in favor of bulimia.") The pro-ana community not only accepts girls in their eating disorders, it also encourages them to continue in their disorders.

Pro-ana sites offer tips and tricks on how to excel at the eating disorder of choice, advice on how to hide it from family and friends, and even pictures of thin and emaciated women to offer inspiration, called "thinsperation." On these sites, *Ana* is not anorexia the life-controlling eating disorder, but a female goddess who promises a thin, fulfilled life in exchange for total devotion and sacrifice to her alone.

> *My friends from the pro-ana sites encourage me to choose my eating disorder. It makes me feel powerful and in control of something that deep down I know I am not. Part of me is captivated by these sites. I am drawn to the acceptance and feel that I belong. The other part of me feels I am falling in a bottomless pit as I live every day off these dark lies.*
>
> —Allie, personal journal entry

Below are examples of statements from a pro-ana site contrasted with promises from God's Word. As you can see, it is clear that you are presented with a choice about what to believe, which we will discuss in more detail in the other chapters of this book.

> *Pro-ana*: "I must be thin and remain thin if I wish to be loved."
> *God's Word*: "All beautiful you are, my darling; there is no flaw in you" (Song of Solomon 4:7).
>
> *Pro-ana*: "Food is my ultimate enemy."
> *God's Word*: "For we are not fighting against flesh-and-blood enemies, but against evil rulers and authorities of

the unseen world, against mighty powers in this dark world, and against evil spirits in the heavenly places" (Ephesians 6:12, NLT).

Pro-ana: "I must think about food every second of every minute, of every hour, of every day."

God's Word: "Fix your thoughts on what is true, and honorable, and right, and pure, and lovely, and admirable. Think about things that are excellent and worthy of praise. Keep putting into practice all you learned and received from me—everything you heard from me and saw me doing. Then the God of peace will be with you" (Philippians 4:8–9, NLT).

Pro-ana: "I must weigh myself every morning and keep that number in my mind throughout the remainder of the day."

God's Word: "Satisfy us in the morning with your unfailing love, so we may sing for joy to the end of our lives" (Psalm 90:14, NLT).

Pro-ana: "Should I be in such a weakened state that I should cave, I will feel guilty and punish myself accordingly for I have failed her [Ana]."

God's Word: "All of us have sinned and fallen short of God's glory. But God treats us much better than we deserve, and because of Christ Jesus, he freely accepts us and sets us free from our sins" (Romans 3:23–24, CEV).

Pro-ana: "It is the most important thing; nothing else matters."

God's Word: "That is why we never give up. Though our bodies are dying, our spirits are being renewed every day. For our present troubles are small and won't last very long. Yet they produce for us a glory that vastly outweighs them and will last forever! So we don't look at the troubles we can see now; rather, we fix our gaze on things that cannot be seen. For the things we see now will soon be gone, but the things we cannot see will last forever" (2 Corinthians 4:16–18, NLT).

Pro-ana: I will devote myself to "Ana"; she will be with me wherever I go.

God's Word: "And be sure of this: I am with you always, even to the end of the age" (Matthew 28:20, NLT).

Pro-ana: "She [Ana] is the only one who cares about me and understands."

God's Word: "From heaven the LORD looks down and sees all mankind; from his dwelling place he watches all who live on earth—he who forms the hearts of all, who considers everything they do" (Psalm 33:13–15).

Pro-ana: "Surely calorie and weight charts will follow me all the days of my life, and I will dwell in the fear of the scales forever."

God's Word: "Surely goodness and mercy shall follow me all the days of my life; and I will dwell in the house of the LORD forever" (Psalm 23:6, NKJV).

The following selections are from a letter supposedly written by Ana herself. The goal of the letter is to inspire and encourage girls in their eating disorders. Read how it contrasts with the inspiration taken from God's letter to you (the Bible) and the promises God gives.

> *Ana*: "You are depressed, obsessed, 'in pain,' hurt, reaching out, but no one will listen. Who cares?! You are deserving; you brought this upon yourself."
>
> *God's Word*: "The LORD is close to the brokenhearted and saves those who are crushed in spirit" (Psalm 34:18).

> *Ana*: "Thoughts of anger, sadness, desperation, and loneliness cease because I take them away and fill your head with methodic calorie counting."
>
> *God's Word*: "You have turned my mourning into joyful dancing. You have taken away my clothes of mourning and clothed me with joy" (Psalm 30:11, NLT).

> *Ana*: "You will always be fat and never will you be as beautiful as they are."
>
> *God's Word*: "Charm is deceptive, and beauty does not last; but a woman who fears the LORD will be greatly praised" (Proverbs 31:30, NLT).

The pro-ana movement has helped illustrate this verse from the Old Testament book of Deuteronomy: "This day I call heaven and earth as witnesses against you that I have set before you life and death, blessings and curses. Now choose life, so that you and your children may live" (30:19). God offers you blessing, but the lies from these sites promise nothing except pain and suffering.

The choice has been laid before you, life or death—and God even gives you the answer. Choose life! In the next chapter, you will read about the steps you can take to receive God's mercy and experience freedom from an eating disorder.

Chapter Two

BREAKING FREE

The Bible is very clear that your body is the temple of the Holy Spirit and that you should honor God with your body (1 Corinthians 6:19–20). Self-starvation, induced vomiting, and gluttony are direct violations of that commandment. Yet knowing that these behaviors are sin should not bring condemnation, but hope! You should be encouraged by the promise that Jesus died for your sins so that you may live free from all bondage. The fact that Jesus died for your freedom is evidence that freedom does exist!

You can go from treatment center to treatment center and excel at the ability to "cope" with an eating disorder, or you can pursue the promise of transformation through Jesus Christ. You can continue living as a victim to your diagnosis, or you can choose to believe what God says about freedom: "Now the Lord is the Spirit and where the Spirit of the Lord is, there is freedom" (2 Corinthians 3:17).

Whatever the root of the eating disorder may be, the solution is far more complex than simply eating balanced meals and keeping the food down. A problem will not go away until the root causes are dealt with. But freedom *is* possible—freedom *does* exist for you! Jesus is the only true source of freedom, and He wants nothing more than to see you experiencing it fully.

Imagine yourself sitting in a classroom full of students. The teacher is standing at the front with an envelope of money. She announces to the class that she has a one-hundred-dollar bill for anyone who is interested. It's not a trick or a bribe, just a gift from the heart of the teacher to bless the lives of her students. However, in order to receive the gift, there are steps you have to take. You must get out of your chair, walk to the front of the room, and stretch out your hand to receive the gift. The same is true with the gift of freedom.

Freedom is yours, but there are steps you must take to receive it. The problem is that there are many hindrances in your way: unforgiveness, the lies of the enemy, debris left by past generations, the pain of past hurts, and oppression from the devil himself. To get to the gift, you have to clear the path! In this chapter we'll look at how to do that. You don't want anything slowing you down from receiving all God has for you.

Choose Love

God loves you unconditionally. He has seen you through your entire struggle and knows better than anyone your internal battle, long sleepless nights, and feelings of hopelessness. There is nothing you have done or could ever do that is beyond God's grace and mercy. He knew the battle you would be fighting and sent His Son, Jesus, to die on the cross with you in mind. The sacrifice Jesus made on the cross and the blood He shed there was for you—to cleanse you of sin, guilt, shame, and condemnation.

If you have never accepted Jesus as your personal Savior, all you have to do is ask. He is quick to forgive and will give you a completely new start. He is eagerly waiting to come into your heart and lead you on a journey to freedom from the bondage you are living in now. Here is a sample prayer you can use:

Prayer for Salvation

Jesus, I am so lost. I don't know how I got so far from you, but I have. I need you, and I ask you to come into my heart. Save me! Change my heart. I believe you are the Son of God; I believe you died on a cross for my sin and shame. This day, I choose life. I choose you. I know that you will walk with me on this journey, so I can rest in knowing that you will help me through it all. In Jesus' name, Amen.

Communicate with God

Accepting Jesus as your Savior and Lord is a wonderful step toward freedom, but simply "getting saved" isn't enough. If you fail to develop a real relationship with God, you will miss out on a lifetime of amazing experiences, blessings, joy, and freedom. The Lord doesn't expect you to be perfect or all put together. He wants to meet you right where you are and pick up the pieces of your broken life. He desires to create a relationship with you that will meet the needs that are driving you to these harmful behaviors.

A good place to start developing a relationship with anyone is by spending time together talking. The Lord wants you to talk to Him, and He desires to talk to you. The most important thing you can ever do in any situation, good or bad, is to share it with God. Cry out to Him in your times of desperation, and rejoice with Him in all your breakthroughs and victories.

You may be thinking, *Wait—the Lord wants to talk to me?* Yes, He does! And not just about important areas where you need His guidance, but about everything. (See Psalm 37:23; 1 Peter 5:7.) When you spend time with the Lord, talking to Him and listening to Him, you will begin to receive the truth and guidance of God for your life!

God wants to hear from you, but He also wants you to listen to Him. He is always speaking, but can you hear His voice? Getting into the Word of God is the best way to begin hearing what He has to say to you. The stronger your relationship with God becomes, the more you will grow, and growing in God is the beginning of your freedom. Not only will you gain freedom from an eating disorder, but also the truth of God's Word sets you completely free in every area of your life.

> *It's such a relief to know God has given me a way out. I can choose not to be a slave to this eating disorder. That does not mean it's easy, though. Daily choosing to walk in freedom is anything but easy, but I am so glad I do not have to do it alone.*
>
> —Allie, personal journal entry

God also will speak to you through the affirmations of others and, although rarely audible, through the Holy Spirit. This is that "still small voice" Christians sometimes refer to, which helps us to decide between right and wrong. "There is something deep within them that echoes God's yes and no, right and wrong" (Romans 2:15, MSG). The problem is, the more you ignore His voice, the harder it is to hear it.

Imagine trying to talk to your best friend with a thick stone wall twenty feet tall between you. It would be very hard for you to hear what your friend had to say and for her to hear you. That wall represents the sin that stands between you and God, a wall you've built with every act of disobedience against Him. The good news is that God will help you tear down the wall! He loves you and doesn't want anything to stand between you and Him. If you can't seem to hear His voice, step back and see what is separating you from God. Ask for forgiveness, and He will gladly help you grow closer to Him. Once there are no barriers, you can begin to listen for God's voice.

Think about your life—what fills most of your time, energy, and thoughts? If it is not the Lord, you may need to reevaluate your priorities. God is listening. He desires to help and bless you. Jeremiah 33:3 says, "Call to me and I will answer you. I'll tell you marvelous and wondrous things that you could never figure out on your own" (MSG).

Accept Responsibility

You have tried everything you know to do to get better through your own strength. Consequently, you have to come to the place where you see your desperate need for God. You have reached the breaking point, and you know that there is nothing and no one else but God who can transform your life. There's a gaping hole in your heart that can only be filled by Him. If you continue to look to anything else to fill that void, you will find yourself lost and unsatisfied.

Now you have to take responsibility for the decisions you have made to participate in the eating disorder behaviors. When you acknowledge that you have a problem, then you can ask God to forgive you for allowing the eating disorder to continue to rule your life. He has already forgiven you, but He is waiting for you to receive His forgiveness. To *repent* means to turn in a new and different direction, away from the sin of the eating disorder. You make the decision to follow after God and live in His truth, free from guilt and condemnation, and then you act on that decision.

> *One significant point was when I finally admitted, realized, and took responsibility for the fact that I have a CHOICE. I did not choose what happened to me as a child and the abuse that I endured, but I finally understood that I had a choice about my future and the life that I would live . . . . Every challenge I faced and every hard memory I had to deal with was a choice for life. I could run away, hide, and remain controlled by pain and fear and keep myself in a life of darkness. Or I could trust God, choose to walk it out, and have life! No one could make the choice for me, and no one could force me into a specific choice. The choice was mine and is continually mine. And I choose LIFE!*
>
> —Allie, personal journal entry

One vital step toward repentance is recognizing that the eating disorder is a sin and that you need God to deliver you from the bondage of it. Choosing the control of an eating disorder is turning away from God and His ability to meet your needs. Repentance is turning back toward Him and allowing Him to do His amazing healing work in your life.

Nothing you've done is too much for God to forgive. He already knows everything about you and everything you have done, and He loves you in spite of it all! His desire is for you to recognize the sin in your life for what it is and to bring it to

Him to forgive. Once God forgives you; your sin is gone! Psalm 103:12 explains, "He has removed our sins as far from us as the east is from the west" (NLT).

By choosing God's love, accepting Jesus as Savior and Lord, giving control of your life to God, refusing to fall for Satan's lies, developing a real relationship with God, taking responsibility for your actions, and repenting of your bad decisions—you are well on your way to breaking free! But freedom is a process, and there are other steps you need to take.

Give and Receive Forgiveness

Another important step to freedom is to forgive those who have hurt you and to receive forgiveness for your mistakes. It has been said that it is impossible to be bitter and get better at the same time. The only person you are hurting by holding onto unforgiveness is yourself. You are actually creating a spiritual tie to the person you refuse to forgive.

Forgiveness is often mistakenly thought to be an emotion. It is easy to forgive others when they apologize or when you are no longer hurt or angry, but what about in the midst of your pain? That is when you have to recognize that forgiveness is a choice, not a feeling or an emotion.

Forgiving others for what they did to hurt you does not make what they did right, nor does it minimize your pain. Your angry and hurt feelings are normal, but you only hurt yourself if you continue to hold onto them.

As you forgive others, you are opening the door to receive God's forgiveness. If you do not forgive others, the Lord cannot extend His forgiveness to you. You have to forgive others if you want Jesus to forgive you. Matthew 6:14–15 says, "If you forgive others for the wrongs they do to you, your Father in heaven will forgive you. But if you don't forgive others, your Father will not forgive your sins" (CEV).

Let God be your vindicator. He sees your hurt and pain, and He will bring justice into your situation. By holding tightly to unforgiveness, you are hindering your walk to freedom. Release it to God, and choose to forgive so He can begin to restore you!

Satan will try to haunt you with the sins of your past. When he brings them back up, remember that God has forgotten your sin. You are a completely new person, no longer bound by the shame of your past. Once you forgive others and receive God's forgiveness in return, you will feel as if a heavy burden has been lifted off of you. That is one more roadblock out of the way!

Here is a sample prayer you can use to help you give and receive forgiveness:

Prayer of Forgiveness

Lord, I come before you right now, and I ask you to first forgive me for holding unforgiveness and bitterness in my heart. I see my need for your healing in my life in this area. Right now I forgive anyone who has ever hurt me for everything they have done that has hurt me. I release them right now, in Jesus' name. I ask, Lord, that you would bless them and that they would come to know you deeply. I choose to forgive right now, even if I don't feel it, because I know your Word says that if I forgive, I will be forgiven.

I also forgive myself for making wrong decisions, for turning from you, Lord, and for holding unforgiveness in my heart. And Lord, I know you never caused any bad thing to happen to me in my life, but I blamed you and I forgive you right now. James 1:17 says, "Every good and perfect gift is from above, coming down from the Father of the heavenly lights, who does not change like shifting shadows." Thank you, Lord, for forgiving me as I have chosen to forgive others. Help me to walk in forgiveness every day. In Jesus' name, Amen.

Believe the Truth

There are so many lies in my head about who I am and what I am worth. My counselor suggested I write out the truths about who God says I am on index cards and start every morning by reading them out loud. I am amazed how, over time, my thinking has changed! The truths I am pouring into my mind are beginning to wash out all of the lies.

—Allie, personal journal entry

The words you speak about yourself, as well as the words others speak over you, have the power to create life or death. When you look in the mirror every day and say, "I am worthless!" you begin to believe that lie.

God's Word is complete truth. Therefore, if something does not align with the Bible, it is not derived from truth. For example, the "pro-ana" web sites promote being thin in order to be loved and beautiful, but nowhere in the Bible can that idea be found.

Satan is a liar (John 8:44). There is no truth in Satan, and there never will be. He lies to you every day about how others view you and what God thinks about you. He magnifies your weaknesses so you begin to lose confidence in yourself, other people, and God. Satan wants nothing more than to lead you to believe that you came from nothing, are nothing, will always be nothing, and are going nowhere. What a lie! He works through people, sometimes even through your parents or peers, to reinforce his lies. If you believe him, it will directly affect your actions, habits, character, and destiny.

Jesus has given His followers authority over the enemy (Luke 10:19). All Satan can do is lie and attempt to convince you to believe his lies. How can you know the difference? The Word of God, the Bible, should always be your definer of truth. You ultimately choose whether you will accept the lies of Satan or believe the Word of God.

Renew Your Mind

The Word of God says that when we renew our minds, our lives will be changed: "Don't copy the behavior and customs of this world, but let God transform you into a new person by changing the way you think. Then you will learn to know God's will for you, which is good and pleasing and perfect" (Romans 12:2, NLT). Renewing your mind means to do away with ungodly thought patterns and to replace them with godly ones. It is impossible to do this without God's help. The world can help you change a behavior, but God helps you change your beliefs and actions, which begins with a change inside the human heart.

For thoughts to become beliefs takes time and repetition. Did you know that memorizing and repeating information have a physical effect on your brain? Scientific experiments seem to indicate that repetitive thoughts over time become physical ruts in the brain that affect your reasoning, choices, and eventually your beliefs. That is why Satan tries so hard to influence what you think. He knows that once you are convinced that your thoughts are true, you will defend your actions even if they are ungodly. Letting the Word of God take charge of your thought life is the only answer to turning your thoughts into a godly belief system that will change your actions to line up with the will of God.

How do you do this? You do this by getting the Word of God into your thought process and letting the power of His truth work. When you put the truth of God's Word into the process of repetitive thoughts and begin to spend more time meditating on that truth than on the lies you have believed, you will see change.

A great way to begin is to write down the lies that you listen to or say every day about who you are and who God is. Then go to the Bible to find the truths that counteract these false beliefs. At the back of this book are some examples to get you started. If you need help finding what you need in the Bible, ask a trusted mature Christian friend to work with you on this. Once you find the truths that God has for you, write them down and begin to speak those truths out loud every day to remove the lies from your mind. Continue this process, and you will begin to see the power of God's Word. As it changes your thoughts, your attitudes will change, and eventually you will see a change in your behaviors.

You may ask, "What if I finally realize the lies I have believed, but it's too hard to keep myself from slipping back into the old way?" You're right—it's not going to be a smooth ride. You will have trials and make mistakes along the way, but that is okay. The key is not how many times you fall but how fast you get back up. The Lord is not as concerned about your falling as He is concerned about your not trying at all.

As a baby learns to walk, her parents do not scold her when she falls; the point is that she is learning and growing. Her parents look at her with great joy, because she has reached this point in her growth. When she falls, they smile, pick her up, and send her on her way to try again until she learns. Even when children have learned to walk, they still fall down sometimes, and adults stumble and trip even though they have been walking for many years. Start renewing your mind, and let God bring forth the transformation you desire. The key is to be faithful and keep growing.

If you are working on building your life for a healthy future, you must have strong supports in place that can withstand the difficulties that will come your way. Philippians 2:13 says, "For God is working in you, giving you the desire and the power to do what pleases him" (NLT). This verse promotes strength and perseverance to keep fighting, because God is fighting next to you. John 15:7 says, "But if you remain in me and my words remain in you, you may ask for anything you want, and it will be granted" (NLT).

Renewing your mind builds a strong foundation for your life. You have to tear down the old and corrupted parts of your mind and behaviors in order to rebuild with the Word of God. The principles of God must be the foundation on which everything in your life is built. "If you work the words into your life, you are like a smart carpenter who dug deep and laid the foundation of his house on bedrock. When the river burst its banks and crashed against the house, nothing could shake it; it was built to last. But if you just use my words in Bible studies and don't work them into your life, you are like a dumb carpenter who built a house but skipped the foundation. When the swollen river came crashing in, it collapsed like a house of cards. It was a total loss" (Luke 6:48–49, MSG).

Here is a sample prayer you can use as you work on renewing your mind with God's truth:

Prayer of Renewal

Lord, according to your Word in Romans 12:1–2, I will choose to present my body to you, God, as a living sacrifice, holy and pleasing to you, and I will no longer allow my body to be used as an instrument of sin. I submit to the process of being transformed by the renewing of my mind. I ask you to "search me [thoroughly], O God, and know my heart! Try me and know my thoughts! And see if there is any wicked or hurtful way in me, and lead me in the way everlasting" (Psalm 139:23–24, AMP).

I ask you to help me in this process. Your Word tells me you created me in your image and that you desire to set me free in my thinking, feelings, and the choices I make. I want to see myself, others, and you the way I should, and without negativity. I ask for your grace to help me cooperate with you as you renew my mind. The blood of Jesus has redeemed me, and I am forgiven! My body is the temple of the Holy Spirit, and I am no longer my own. I belong to you (1 Corinthians 6:19). Thank you for loving me when I have not been able to love myself. As I submit myself to this process, I thank you that I will have victory. In Jesus' name, Amen!

Break the Curse

Generational sins are patterns of specific sins that have been repeated throughout the generations in your family line. (Generational sins are also sometimes called generational curses.) As the disobedience of your family has affected you, so your own actions will affect the generations ahead of you. God promises blessings when you choose to obey His Word, but disobedience will only lead to more heartache in your life, as well as in the lives of your children and grandchildren.

Take time to identify the issues in your family that could cause difficulty. A few examples are depression, anger, addictions, pride, sexual sins, abuse, fear, manipulation, and emotional dependency. Once you have identified the struggles, pray and ask God to break these patterns and sins in your life. Jesus has given you the authority to break these curses from previous generations so that you can pass on blessings to those who follow you. Here is a sample prayer you can use:

Prayer to Break Generational Patterns

Father God, I thank you that I do not have to live a life patterned after the generations before me and their sin. I thank you that through Jesus I have the authority to break the generational sins of _____. I choose to forgive my parents and ancestors, releasing any feelings of bitterness or resentment for the consequences that their sin had on my life. I ask you to forgive me for giving in to temptation and yielding to the sin. I receive your forgiveness and choose to move forward. I will no longer live in the shame of my wrong choices. In Jesus' name, Amen.

Chapter Three

STAYING FREE

Satan is a thief, and he has tried to steal something from you—your life! It is okay to be angry about that. God sure is! In fact, He is so disgusted with what Satan is trying to do to His beloved children that He allowed His Son, Jesus, to die an excruciating death to give you authority over the devil. Use that authority you have been given, and fight back!

You can say out loud to the devil, "In the name of Jesus, I demand that you get away from me! I will no longer believe your lies, and I choose to believe the truth of the Word of God!" Satan has to listen and obey (James 4:7). The Bible also says, in James 2:19, "You believe that there is one God. Good for you! Even the demons believe this, and they tremble in terror" (NLT). Even the demons know the authority that comes with using the name of Jesus.

Matthew 10:1 says, "Jesus summoned His twelve disciples and gave them authority over unclean spirits, to cast them out, and to heal every kind of disease and every kind of sickness" (NASB). If you have accepted Jesus as your Lord and Savior, then you also are one of His disciples, and you have been given the same power and authority that Jesus gave the original twelve. Use your authority and claim your freedom!

Identify Your Focus

Freedom from an eating disorder is your goal, but that shouldn't be your focus. When you focus on the *problem*, you can't see the solution. God is the answer to the freedom you are seeking, and He should be your main focus.

When an eating disorder is all that you have known, setting your focus on God rather than food is not something that comes easily. Begin by choosing to focus your thoughts on God every morning when you wake up. This may feel unnatural, so use some resources to help you. Read God's Word, and listen to some praise and worship music; praise God for who He is. Go outside and admire His creation.

Identifying your focus first thing each day is a great start, but maintaining your focus throughout the day may be difficult. Sporadically during the day, you may need to purposefully refocus your thoughts, attitudes, and out-of-control emotions back onto God. Take a moment to do this, as often as you need, until it becomes a normal reaction to keep your thoughts centered on Him. Thoughts of the eating disorder will eventually lose their power to control your actions and will become less overwhelming.

Philippians 4:8 says, "Whatever things are true, whatever things are noble, whatever things are just, whatever things are pure, whatever things are lovely, whatever things are of good report, if there is any virtue and if there is anything praiseworthy—meditate on these things" (NKJV). Meditating on things that are true, just, pure, lovely, and of good report may require some change in your lifestyle. The movies and television shows you watch affect your mind. Magazines that picture extremely thin models are not considered praiseworthy material. Make a list of the things you watch, read, and listen to that you recognize are distractions from your primary focus.

Be encouraged! As you begin to put your focus on God and His love for you, the struggles, torment, and bondage of the eating disorder will seem to fade away.

Develop Godly Routines

Eating disorders can be very ritualistic by nature. You may have formed unhealthy patterns and habits related to an eating disorder without even realizing it. Replacing your distorted thoughts with God's truth is very important, but it is equally important to replace your old eating disorder patterns with new godly routines.

> *I always ate alone. If I was with someone, I didn't want to talk or carry on a conversation, just focus on staying in control. All I want is for a meal to be just that—a meal. I want a meal to be about the people I am with, not the food I am eating. I started slowly, by eating with someone I trusted and playing a word game. Once I became comfortable with that, we tried to have actual conversations; then eventually I could eat around more people. It is a slow process, but I know what my goal is, and I am working toward it.*
>
> —Allie, personal journal entry

The first step is identifying your unhealthy routines or patterns. Some bad habits may seem so normal to you that an outside perspective from someone you trust may be needed to help you see them. Then begin to replace these patterns with healthy behaviors. This may seem very frightening and require additional support from a trusted friend or family member.

Be specific about the goals you are working toward and the steps you are taking to reach them. Routines that include isolating yourself from others need to be quickly identified and replaced. Do this by surrounding yourself with people who know and love God and who speak truth into your life.

If your daily routine includes large amounts of time on the computer participating in pro-ana sites or reading magazines and books that focus on appearance, these activities also need to be replaced. Find books that focus on hobbies you enjoy or Christian books filled with truth. Get involved in a church and make church-related activities a priority.

Another routine you may want to establish is prayer before meals, asking God to give you strength as you face something new and challenging or to give you wisdom to know what a healthy amount of food is.

An eating disorder can quickly control your lifestyle, so creating an entirely new life is never easy, especially if your physical environment has not changed. It will take a large amount of effort on your part, combined with outside support, but freedom is worth any necessary sacrifice.

Choose Your Relationships

The power of choice can be applied to every aspect of your life, including relationships. Many relationships in your life may be due to convenience. You hang out with people from work or school because you have the same schedules, or you grow close to your neighbors because they are only a few steps away. It is normal to develop friendships with the people you are surrounded by. The key is to carefully choose the individuals with whom you develop a close relationship. Look at the person and ask yourself some honest questions:

- Is this person currently in a growing relationship with God?
- Does he or she exhibit behaviors and actions that reflect a relationship with God?
- Does this person encourage my relationship with God and hold me accountable for my actions?
- What has God told me about my relationship with this person through His Holy Spirit, the Word, or Christian counsel?

You may feel like you are automatically thrown or forced into a relationship with the people you are surrounded by, especially in a work or school situation. While reflecting Christ and His love to everyone is always important, sometimes you have to look outside your comfort zone to find healthy relationships. The truth is that you choose who you spend your time with outside of work or school. Choose wisely, knowing that the people around you are playing an intricate role in your path to freedom without their even knowing it.

Close the Door

Closing the door to an eating disorder involves taking daily practical steps to prevent old thoughts, habits, or patterns from taking control of your life again. Acting on the following tips will not come naturally and will require consistent repetition and support to become a normal part of your everyday life, but they will have a tremendous impact on your progress toward freedom.

Closing the Door to Anorexia

Seek advice from a counselor or nutritionist as you set appropriate guidelines.

- Visit with a nutritionist to learn what your meals should consist of and to identify healthy portion sizes.
- Challenge yourself daily with an uncomfortable food or with breaking a routine.
- Limit eating alone.
- Set a daily exercise limit.
- Remove any scales from your home.
- Post scriptures about your identity in Christ on all your mirrors; read them every time you look in the mirror and before focusing on your appearance.
- Journal your thoughts and emotions daily.
- Identify your ungodly beliefs, and replace them with God's truth; write out the truth, and read it aloud until you believe it.

Closing the Door to Bulimia

Seek advice from a counselor or nutritionist as you set appropriate guidelines.

- Visit with a nutritionist to learn what your meals should consist of and to identify healthy portion sizes.

- Do not skip meals.
- Establish an accountability person before every meal who will remain available for an extended period of time after you eat.
- Limit eating alone.
- Remove the scales from your home.
- Limit time spent alone.
- Post scriptures about your identity in Christ in your bathroom and on all your mirrors; read them every time you enter the bathroom or look in the mirror.
- Journal your thoughts and emotions daily, especially after meals.
- Identify your ungodly beliefs, and replace them with God's truth; write out the truth, and read it aloud until you believe it.

Closing the Door to a Binge-Eating Disorder

Seek advice from a counselor or nutritionist as you set appropriate guidelines.

- Visit with a nutritionist to learn what your meals should consist of and to identify healthy portion sizes.
- For each meal, set out exactly what you will be eating, and limit yourself to that amount.
- Limit eating alone.
- Remove the scales from your home.
- Limit time spent alone.

- Post scriptures about your identity in Christ on all your mirrors; read them aloud every time you look in the mirror.
- Journal your thoughts and emotions daily, especially after meals.
- Identify your ungodly beliefs, and replace them with God's truth; write out the truth, and read it aloud until you believe it.

The Temple

Your body is the temple of God (1 Corinthians 6:19–20) and needs to be treated as such. Learning how to eat balanced portions is important, but the choices you make and the foods you eat are equally important. In our modern world, what is called "food" can be filled with preservatives and chemicals that can cause as much long-term damage as the effects of an eating disorder, so seek out nutritional advice from someone who understands the need to eat nutritionally sound food. *The Great Physician's Rx for Women's Health* by Jordan and Nicki Rubin is an excellent nutritional resource. The authors provide a better understanding of these principles and empower you to make healthy choices to reclaim your body as the temple of God. For additional information, visit their web site at www. biblicalhealthinstitute.com.

Chapter Four

STORIES OF MERCY

*I*t can be easy to *say* that you desire healing. Who does not want to be free from living in pain and suffering? The question is, are you trying to gain freedom in your own strength or in the strength God gives?

In order to receive complete restoration, you must surrender entirely to God. James 4:7 clearly states, "Surrender to God! Resist the devil, and he will run from you" (CEV). Many times we trust God, going through the motions, but continue to rely on ourselves rather than His ability in us. If this is your situation, the freedom you experience will be temporary. True heart change is the only way freedom can be maintained.

A heart change occurs when you realize who you are in Christ and how great and unconditional His love is for you. It's not that you know it just in your mind, but that you also recognize it and believe it in your heart. You personally experience that Christ is real and that He lives in you. If you know this and believe this, then you can walk out your freedom in the strength God gives. When you reach this point, you will remain free from the eating disorder, because you have received the revelation that your body is the temple of the Holy Spirit, and God lives in you—and you lose the desire to starve or binge or purge. You actually begin to appreciate your body and to care for it.

True heart change—transformation—comes from understanding that the blood of Christ has cleansed you and that God's mercy and grace (His undeserved favor) is a gift. Neither of these is something you earn or deserve. There is nothing you can do to attain freedom outside of receiving it from the Lord. Realize you can do nothing, be nothing, and say nothing that will produce permanent freedom in your life apart from God's mercy and grace. When you experience and begin to live a transformed life, it is because you are grounded in the Word and surrendered in your relationship with God. Nothing will be able to shake that foundation.

In secular treatment, the focus is on changing behavior, which is only temporary. There may be structure, support, and counseling, but there is no heart change. Behavior modification is not the answer; it is only an outward change, not an inward transformation.

God is the answer. Why? As you surrender to Him, He can change your heart and your desires. He is able to help you, because He created you. If you leave God out and try to attain freedom in your own strength, you will be greatly frustrated and will continually battle with an eating disorder.

Satan's plan for you is destruction, but Jesus came that you might have abundant life. In Him all things are possible. He knew you before you were even in your mother's womb. He has a plan for you (Jeremiah 29:11; John 10:10). He sees your potential and has hope for you to reach that potential. He created you and knows that you are able to fulfill your purpose on this earth, but only through Him can you do it. Walk with the God who made you and knows you better than you could ever know yourself. Let Him walk you through this journey.

Brooklyn and Nicole are two girls who were entangled in the bondage of eating disorders. They both achieved freedom through Jesus and finding their identity in Him. An eating disorder does not have to be something you struggle with for the rest of your life. God graciously extends His hand to anyone willing to receive it. He is willing to do the very same for you. These girls tell their story of how God pulled them out of deception and set them free. These girls chose life, and you can make the same choice. May their stories of mercy bring you hope!

Brooklyn's Story

I grew up in a loving Christian home, but I felt pressure to always measure up and meet a standard I felt was placed in front of me. From a very young age, I was very concerned with my appearance. When I was around five years old, I can remember having nightmares of a man holding a gun to my head and telling me I had to eat a cookie. I never told anyone about these dreams, thinking they were normal. I did not realize this was abnormal, as I assumed every child had these feelings about food.

As I got older, my preoccupation with food, weight, and appearance only got stronger. By middle school, I was determined to be skinny, even though I was not overweight. I thought becoming anorexic was the only way I could obtain the thinness I desired. Even as I desired to be anorexic, I never thought that it would control my life.

Around this time, I began seriously testing the waters of eating disorders. I began fasting off and on, just to see how long I could go without food. After giving in to the hunger that consumed me, I attempted to make myself vomit to get rid of the guilt and feeling of failure. At first it was not easy for me, and in my skewed sense of achievement, I was frustrated that

I was not good at purging. The feelings of guilt and disgust with myself motivated me to continue to purge, until it soon became part of my everyday life.

By high school, I was fully entangled in the lies, depression, anger, and pure distortion that tend to accompany eating disorders. My mental state began to affect my performance at school, and I went from being a straight-A student to not going to classes in order to act out in the eating disorder. I hated life. I hated God for letting me live, even though deep inside of me I knew He was my only answer. Hospitals, doctors, dieticians, therapists, and psychiatrists became part of my everyday life. I was in and out of treatment centers, and with each discharge I felt more and more hopeless.

During this time I also added binge-eating (followed by purging) into my life. I had learned about bulimia in a treatment center. During my struggle with bulimia, I felt more hopeless than ever. My eyes were beginning to open to how out of control I really was. I made it through only two days of my senior year of high school, and then I was hospitalized again. I found myself in another psychiatric unit where they dealt with eating disorders.

Desperate and broken, I applied to Mercy Ministries. I stayed in treatment until it was time to go to Mercy. When I got there, I knew it was where I was supposed to be, but I honestly did not believe I would make it through the program. I knew I didn't have any other options, but somehow I thought that God's love and the freedom I was being told about was for everyone but me. I hated myself, so my actions reflected that self-hatred. I continued to act out in the destructive eating patterns.

After a while, I slowly started allowing God to change my thinking through reading the Bible and speaking truth over myself. It was a very hard process for me, because it required trust. Over time, I started to accept that God had made me for more than what I had thus far experienced, and that He was concerned about me. That revelation changed my life, because I had always felt unheard and that no one truly cared about me.

When I graduated from the program at Mercy, I was a new woman. That is not to say that I am not tempted by the old behaviors, but in the midst of my struggles I am learning that it is possible to live a healthy, balanced life, as long as I daily rely on God.

By the grace of God, I have now completed a semester of college! I used to believe Satan's lie that I would be dead by now, or that if I lived I would never accomplish anything and would always be worthless. This semester has been proof that God is with me and leading me. He is teaching me that not only can I function in life—I can live! God has given me freedom, and I am choosing to walk in it daily!

Nicole's Story

Growing up, I was the perfect child with the perfect life. I grew up in a loving Christian home with status and wealth, but money never bought my happiness or healing. I knew there had to be something more.

I started to flirt with an eating disorder in the fourth grade, yet I never restricted enough to lose a drastic amount of weight. I had roots of rejection and low self esteem from a young age. I was bullied and constantly teased by people that I trusted and called my friends. I was a perfectionist, requiring everything from great grades to outfits matching to a tee. Anytime that

I didn't measure up to my ever-changing standard, self-hatred manifested in me. Because of my perfectionism, I believed the lie that no one would accept me with weaknesses or faults, so I tried to act like I did not have any, wearing various masks to cover these various hurts. Because I wore these masks for so long, I had no idea who I really was. I was also very performance-based, believing that what I did defined who I was.

Of course I had a lot of control issues and loved being in control of anything and everything, including my weight. This obsession landed me in a doctor's office after my mom had seen me in a swim suit and realized that there had to be something wrong. My eyes were sunken, and I had extra hair all over my body, giving me a skeleton-like look. I convinced both my family and myself that I was fine. This denial continued for about a year, until I realized that something was wrong, and I finally admitted that I did have an eating disorder.

Deeply troubled, I told my family, and we decided together that if anorexia was not eating, then freedom was simply to eat. So I started eating and gained a couple of pounds. This made my family happy and convinced them once again that everything was okay. I continued like this for three more years, eating just enough to make everyone think I was okay, while still covering up the deep pain buried within. The pain came out in other ways, however, such as depression, self-harm, and suicide attempts.

Along with being anorexic, I had an extreme exercise obsession that controlled my life. Every waking moment, if I wasn't thinking about how not to eat, counting calories, or planning my next meal, then I was working out. I was still left unfulfilled, and I turned to the one thing I had not yet tried . . . bulimia.

I know now that God was protecting me as a result of the prayers of others, but no matter how hard I tried, I just could not make myself throw up. I decided that if God was so powerful in stopping me, then I would turn to the devil to help me. I renounced God and all He stood for and started praying to Satan daily to help me become bulimic. Satan gladly took this opportunity, and soon I was living in hell on earth. Those I loved the most turned away from me, feeling helpless and scared by my choices.

Not only did the eating disorder fail to fulfill any need in me, but also it left me more miserable than ever. I began to understand why God had tried to protect me from this misery. I wanted out and cried out to God in desperation. I knew He was my only hope of obtaining freedom. I was deep in the eating disorder and felt completely powerless. I had to go through a process that included more bad days than good days at first. I had to dig up the roots of what led to my current state, feel them, face them, and then replace them with the unconditional love of God. It was a painful process! But by continuing to do that and pressing through the pain, I found myself so full of truth that there was no room for lies.

I know God loves me no matter what I've done or will do, and that I'm worthy to hear from Him. He accepts me for who I really am. I am beautiful, and I don't have to be prefect to be loved. The most important thing to me was realizing that I didn't have to live with an eating disorder the rest of my life! There is actual freedom in Christ!

Chapter Five

FOR PARENTS AND OTHERS WHO CARE

Today another doctor told me Allie would be battling an eating disorder the rest of her life. Although it's easy to feel discouraged and look at that statement as truth, I know it has to be a lie. I refuse to believe that an eating disorder is too big for God. The problem is, I can't do it for her. I can lead her to the truth, but I have to accept that it is her choice. Right now, my job as a mother is to pray.

—Allie's mother, personal journal entry

*Y*ou may be a parent, mentor, pastor, or friend of someone struggling with an eating disorder and are uncertain of how to best offer support. Hopefully, as you read this book, you will find some answers to assist you in helping your loved one and your family.

Effective communication, building a healthy relationship with your daughter, and knowing your role as a support person in her life are vital. The causes and effects of anorexia, bulimia, and binge-eating disorders can be intrinsically linked to the support system as a whole. Although your daughter is the one suffering with the eating disorder, those around her are also affected in negative ways. Families tend to be greatly affected by the disorder, but any type of support can assist in fostering healing and help those who are hurting.

It is crucial for the whole family to seek help together for the situation you are facing. Avoiding your daughter or detaching from her issue is an ineffective approach—ignoring the facts will not make them disappear. It is important to keep in mind that an eating disorder is not solely about food. Confronting the roots of what is happening with your daughter and in your family is what will bring about resolution.

> *I've been silently observing my daughter for a while, but I can't be silent anymore. She refused to eat again tonight, and I lost my cool. I began to yell, and then I broke down into sobs. It's a constant battle between a frustrated anger and a compassionate heart. I am beginning to realize that she needs more help than I can give her.*
>
> —Allie's mother, personal journal entry

As a caring parent, your first step must be to pray and seek God for wisdom in supporting your daughter. While many circumstances are out of your control, prayer and guidance are within your control. Supportive confrontation, without judgment, is the best way to foster positive change in your daughter's life; she needs to know that you love her regardless of her behavior.

The Bible says that love never fails (1 Corinthians 13:8). When your approach and concern for your daughter come from the unconditional love and leading of the Holy Spirit, you will begin to see results that are long lasting. Approach your daughter with compassion and open communication, and let God lead you throughout the whole process of healing.

Communicate Effectively

Creating and maintaining open communication with your daughter is essential for a healthy relationship. Communication is not merely about talking to someone or showing interest; communication is about connecting with another human being in a way that creates an avenue for honesty and change.

The way we communicate, verbally or nonverbally, affects how our message is relayed and received. Girls who struggle with eating disorders often have experienced communication barriers within their families. These barriers can result from fear of intimacy, family secrets, unspoken family rules, avoidance, denial related to public image, and unhealthy family traditions of communication. Seek guidance from the Holy Spirit to enable you to effectively engage with your daughter and to demonstrate the love and honesty necessary for restoration and healing.

Active listening is a major key to effective communication. Being an active listener entails giving the other person your full attention when she is communicating, rather than thinking ahead to what you will say next. When your daughter is talking but you are focused on what you will say next, you are missing vital information that could help you respond to her in the most appropriate manner. Giving your daughter your undivided attention conveys that you love her, support her, and believe her thoughts and feelings are important. And there may be times when your daughter really does not want or need feedback. She may simply want you to listen and hear her heart.

A goal of effective communication is to nurture growth and transparency, while removing walls that block the flow of honest conversation. Some common communication blockers to be aware of before opening dialogue with your daughter are interrupting, ignoring, sarcasm, name-calling, insulting, judging, blaming, and stating your opinion as fact. Open communication in the family lowers the chance of anxious or negative feelings being expressed or repressed in negative ways. Preaching to your daughter while she is hurting could build a wall and prevent her from being honest with you. Consider hearing her out and allowing her to express her emotions. Encouraging your daughter to be aware of her feelings and to express them to you openly will empower honesty and vulnerability, and it is beneficial for you to set an example by being open with her about your own feelings.

Build a Strong Relationship

Your relationship with your daughter is such an important aspect of her finding healing and freedom—it actually can help her realize who God created her to be. By providing her with a foundation of love and open communication, you help her develop confidence and an understanding of how to have healthy relationships with others. Effective communication is vital on your daughter's path to freedom from the eating disorder, and investing in your relationship with her will help her sustain that freedom.

It's very important to communicate your love to your daughter by expressing how unique and exceptional she is in specific areas of her life. Identify and relay to her the strengths and talents you see in her, and take time to encourage her in those areas. Provide verbal encouragement as well as continued training and classes to help her develop her gifts and areas of strength. You'll also want to encourage and help facilitate her seeking spiritual growth in God. When the focus is on her strengths, positive attitudes and behaviors will result, and as all the members of the family provide each other with support and encouragement to maximize their potential, joy and fulfillment will follow.

Be aware that messages about your daughter's weaknesses and inadequacies could be continually running through her mind like a broken record. She may think or feel that she does not measure up to your expectations. You may have never spoken negative words to her, but the enemy is focused on keeping your daughter trapped in the eating disorder and he uses negative thoughts or beliefs. These thoughts and beliefs may have varied sources, but the results have led into disordered eating.

There is an enemy who wants to destroy your daughter and your family. You will need to fight the enemy by speaking the Word of God and affirmation into your daughter's life. Fighting the enemy requires a relationship with God in order to stand firm. Decide that you will fight for your family and yourself. Keeping your own life healthy and whole will help as you assist your daughter in her process of healing and wholeness.

An important aspect of effective communication is conflict resolution. You will need to approach conflict with the understanding that the fight is not with your daughter but with the spiritual attack behind the eating disorder she struggles with. Peaceful resolution involves honest, supportive confrontation. Sometimes families expect everyone to play peacekeeper. As long as everyone avoids confrontation, a kind of peace is present, but this method of operating avoids ever addressing the issue. Avoiding issues will not bring peace; facing issues head-on with a peaceful disposition is what brings about lasting peace.

Confrontation is not easy for most people. It should not be fueled by anger and unforgiveness but by love and genuine forgiveness. Pray before going into any conflict, choosing to forgive those involved, and then proceed with a calm attitude. Through prayer, forgiveness, and thoughtful consideration, you increase the chance for a positive result.

Practical Ways to Build Your Relationship

- Love unconditionally.
- Spend quality time with your daughter. Connect with her by finding ways to interact with her and engage her.
- Attend church together.
- Treat your daughter with respect. Talk about her strengths.
- Be a good listener; don't always give feedback.
- Consistency yields security. Be consistent in your expectations and your parameters.
- Emphasize enjoyment of activities rather than performance.
- Encourage your daughter to take control of important aspects of her life and to make her own decisions when appropriate. Don't be afraid to provide appropriate limits; being too restrictive or too permissive can both have a negative effect.
- Show your daughter how to successfully resolve conflict.
- Be aware of media messages regarding women's bodies, and be open to healthy discussions about these.

Learn How to Provide Support

Your daughter needs your love and support to overcome the eating disorder, but it is also important to address your own needs as a parent. Watching someone you love battle this life-threatening disorder can be a very emotionally challenging experience; no one should walk this road alone. Utilize the support of a caring pastor, Christian counselor, or trusted friends to help you during this difficult time. It is important for you and your daughter that you have a safe place where you can vent, express, and have a chance to work through your own feelings. Allow others to help you as you help the one you love. Feelings are a normal part of being human. It is important to acknowledge your feelings and handle them in the best ways possible.

The tumultuous emotions you feel toward your daughter, the eating disorder, and the effects of the disorder on your family are not uncommon. But with the gamut of emotions you experience, you may become distracted from the truth of God's Word. Encourage yourself with the truth that emotions are fleeting, but the Word of God stands forever (Isaiah 40:8). The Word of God will empower you to stand in the face of adversity and overcome it.

Anger is a common reaction for parents of girls battling an eating disorder. You may feel anger at the disorder, your daughter, yourself, or even at failed treatment attempts, counselors, and institutions. Ephesians 4:26 says, "Be angry and yet do not sin; do not let the sun go down on your anger" (NASB). Your feeling of anger is not sinful. It is how you proceed in that anger that is crucial.

You may also encounter fear about the dangers of an eating disorder and what may happen to your daughter if she continues this destructive behavior. Remember that the Word of God says, "God did not give us a spirit of timidity, but a spirit of power, of love and of self-discipline" (2 Timothy 1:7). Ask God to help you step out of fear as He guides your steps during this time.

In addition to anger and fear, anxiety can be a daily struggle as you deal with questions concerning the effects of the eating disorder on your daughter's life and future. Philippians 4:6–7 says, "Do not be anxious about anything, but in everything, by prayer and petition, with thanksgiving, present your requests to God. And the peace of God, which transcends all understanding, will guard your hearts and your minds in Christ Jesus." Giving God your anxiety and being honest with Him about your petitions releases that anxiety from your life.

Helplessness is another emotion you may experience if you find yourself overwhelmed by your daughter's pain and the realization that you are unable to stop the cycle. Scripture instructs us, "Trust in the LORD with all your heart and lean not on your own understanding; in all your ways acknowledge him, and he will make your paths straight" (Proverbs 3:5–6). Trust means literally choosing to surrender those things that are out of your control, allowing God to lead you during this time.

I feel I have failed as a parent. What have I done wrong that would cause my daughter to fall into such deception? I don't know how to reach her and am looking for something or someone to blame. I don't know where else to go but on my knees.

—Allie's mother, personal journal entry

Unconditional love and support will make a positive difference on your daughter's road to healing and freedom. Seek the Lord for yourself, and find refuge in prayer. Resist the temptation to blame yourself for your daughter's struggles. Although no parent is perfect, the eating disorder is not your fault, and getting stuck in the trap of self-blame will not help your daughter find healing. Understand that there is a difference between taking an objective look at unhealthy family patterns and placing blame on your family. The Word of God teaches us to take responsibility for our mistakes and to receive God's forgiveness (1 John 1:9). It also teaches us that the real battle is not against people but against spiritual darkness (Ephesians 6:12). This is the time to get to the source of the pain and defeat it through Christ.

Remember, there is hope. Here at Mercy, we have seen hundreds of girls and their families receive healing and freedom from eating disorders. These young women have gone on to live productive lives as teachers, businesswomen, ministers, and mothers, sharing their testimonies of healing and bringing hope to others. God is both willing and able to help your family through this journey. He is a God who loves to turn tragedy into triumph. He can take all the pain and suffering your family has experienced and turn it into a story of hope for others.

> *I am watching in awe as the chains fall off my daughter. The process is slow, but God is so faithful! Her freedom is not coming from seeking freedom itself, but from seeking God, the source of freedom. Some days are harder than others, but as we both continue to trust God and seek truth, we know the battle has been won!*
> —Allie's mother, personal journal entry

A Parent's Prayer

Lord, I thank you for my daughter, _____, and the precious gift she is to me. I come to you with a heart of surrender concerning her. You created her and know her more intimately than I do. Although it is hard to comprehend, I know that my love for my daughter does not begin to compare to how much you love her. She is yours, first and foremost, and I trust her to your care.

Protect her and her body during this time. Give me the wisdom to know what to say to her and when to say it, when I need to intervene and when I need to stand back. Forgive me for any attempts to try to "fix her" or save her or make things better in my own strength, and help me to trust her solely to you.

Reveal to me any behavior or attitudes on my part that have contributed to my daughter's eating disorder; show me anything I need to change. Enable me to be more patient and understanding so I can recognize that the true battle is with Satan, not food. I pray for strength as I team with my daughter to fight the spiritual forces at work in this situation. I also ask that you bring physical healing to my daughter's body. In Jesus' name, Amen.

CHANGING UNGODLY BELIEFS TO GODLY BELIEFS

Ungodly Belief: I am unlovable and unworthy. If you knew the real me, you would reject me. No one really likes me.

Godly Belief: With God's help, I can learn to be myself and trust Him to bring people into my life who will appreciate me and respect me for who I am. My worth is in who God says I am.

Truth from the Bible

What's the price of two or three pet canaries? Some loose change, right? But God never overlooks a single one. And he pays even greater attention to you, down to the last detail—even numbering the hairs on your head! So don't be intimidated by all this bully talk. You're worth more than a million canaries.

—Luke 12:6–7, MSG

God rescued us from dead-end alleys and dark dungeons. He's set us up in the kingdom of the Son he loves so much, the Son who got us out of the pit we were in, got rid of the sins we were doomed to keep repeating.

—Colossians 1:13–14, MSG

Ungodly Belief: Even when I do my best, it's not good enough. I can never meet the standard.

Godly Belief: I am fully loved, completely accepted, and totally pleasing to God. Regardless of how much I do or fail to do, I will remain fully loved, completely accepted, and totally pleasing to God. I choose to surrender to Him, trusting my faith in Him and His ability to sustain me. I will seek to be a God pleaser, not a people pleaser.

Truth from the Bible

For I can do everything through Christ, who gives me strength.

—Philippians 4:13, NLT

Seek the Kingdom of God above all else, and live righteously, and he will give you everything you need.

—Matthew 6:33, NLT

Ungodly Belief: My life has been and always will be full of turmoil. Some of my best years have been wasted, and I have no hope.

Godly Belief: God will restore all the time I have wasted or lost by my choices or the choices of others. God gives me peace.

Truth from the Bible

I will restore to you the years that the swarming locust has eaten, the crawling locust, the consuming locust, and the chewing locust.

—Joel 2:25, NKJV

Peace I leave with you, My peace I give to you; not as the world gives do I give to you. Let not your heart be troubled, neither let it be afraid.

—John 14:27, NKJV

INDEX TO PRAYERS

REFERENCES

Nancy Alcorn, *Keys to Walking in Freedom* CD series Mercy
  Ministries
  www.mercyministries.com
Neil T. Anderson, *The Bondage Breaker*
  www.ficm.org
Neil T. Anderson, *The Steps to Freedom in Christ*
  www.ficm.org
Charles Capps, *God's Creative Power*
  www.charlescapps.com
Chester and Betsy Kylstra, *Restoring the Foundations*
  www.phw.org
Jordan and Nicki Rubin, *The Great Physicians RX for Women's
  Health*
  www.jordanrubin.com

ABOUT MERCY MINISTRIES

Mercy Ministries exists to allow young women to experience God's unconditional love, forgiveness, and life-transforming power. We provide residential programs free of charge to young women ages 13–28 who are dealing with life-controlling issues such as eating disorders, self-harm, addictions, sexual abuse, unplanned pregnancy, and depression. Our approach addresses the underlying roots of these issues by addressing the whole person—spiritual, physical, and emotional—and produces more than just changed behavior; the Mercy Ministries program changes hearts and stops destructive cycles.

Founded in 1983 by Nancy Alcorn, Mercy Ministries currently operates in four U.S. states and in Australia, Canada, New Zealand, Peru, and the UK, with plans for additional U.S. and international locations underway. We are blessed to have connecting relationships with many different Christian congregations but are not affiliated with any church, organization, or denomination.

Residents enter Mercy Ministries on a voluntary basis and stay an average of six months. Our program includes life-skills training and educational opportunities that help ensure the success of our graduates. Our goal is to have each young woman not only complete the program but also discover the purpose for her life and bring value to her community as a productive citizen.

STARVED

For more information, visit our Web site at
www.mercyministries.com.

Mercy Ministries of America

www.mercyministries.com

Mercy Ministries Australia

www.mercyministries.com.au

Mercy Ministries Canada

www.mercycanada.com

Mercy Ministries UK

www.mercyministries.co.uk

Mercy Ministries New Zealand

www.mercyministries.org.nz

ABOUT THE AUTHOR

After eight years in corrections and social work, Nancy Alcorn began to realize the inadequacy of secular programs to offer real transformation in the lives of troubled girls.

Believing that only Jesus could bring restoration into the lives of girls who were desperately hurting, she knew God was calling her to step out to do something about it.

In 1983, Nancy opened the first Mercy Ministries home in Monroe, Louisiana. God had instructed her to do three specific things to ensure His blessings on the ministry: to accept girls into the program free of charge, to give at least 10 percent of all Mercy Ministries' donations to other Christian organizations and ministries, and to take no state or federal funding that might limit freedom to teach Christian principles. As Nancy has continued to be faithful to these three principles, God has been faithful to provide for every need of the ministry—just as He promised.

Nancy frequently speaks at conferences around the world. She lives in Nashville, Tennessee, which is also the home of the international headquarters of Mercy Ministries.

To order additional copies of this title call:
1-877-421-READ (7323)
or please visit our web site at
www.winepressbooks.com

If you enjoyed this quality custom published book,
drop by our web site for more books and information.

www.winepressgroup.com
"Your partner in custom publishing."